The Colors We Eat

Red Foods

Patricia Whitehouse

Heinemann Library
Chicago, Illinois

© 2002 Reed Educational & Professional Publishing
Published by Heinemann Library,
an imprint of Reed Educational & Professional Publishing,
Chicago, Illinois

Customer Service 888-454-2279
Visit our website at www.heinemannlibrary.com

Designed by Sue Emerson, Heinemann Library
Printed and bound in the U.S.A. by Lake Book

06 05 04 03 02
10 9 8 7 6 5 4 3 2 1

Library of Congress Cataloging-in-Publication Data
Whitehouse, Patricia, 1958-
   Red foods / Patricia Whitehouse.
       p. cm. — (The colors we eat)
Includes index.
Summary: Introduces things to eat and drink that are red, from apples to pomegranates.
   ISBN: 1-58810-536-9 (HC), 1-58810-744-2 (Pbk.)
   1. Food—Juvenile literature. 2. Red—Juvenile literature. [1. Food.
   2. Red.] I. Title.
TX355 .W47 2002
641.3—dc21

                            2001004796

Acknowledgments
The author and publishers are grateful to the following for permission to reproduce copyright material:
Title page, pp. 5, 6, 17 Greg Beck/Fraser Photos; pp. 4, 7, 12, 16, 18, 19 Michael Brosilow/Heinemann Library;
p. 8 Rick Wetherbee; p. 9 Wally Eberhart/Visuals Unlimited; pp. 10, 15 Dwight Kuhn; p. 11 Amor Montes de Oca;
pp. 13, 14 D. Cavagnaro/Visuals Unlimited; pp. 20L, 20R, 21 Craig Mitchelldyer Photography

Cover photograph courtesy of Greg Beck/Fraser Photos

Every effort has been made to contact copyright holders of any material reproduced in this book.
Any omissions will be rectified in subsequent printings if notice is given to the publisher.

Special thanks to our advisory panel for their help in the preparation of this book:
Eileen Day, Preschool Teacher
Chicago, IL

Paula Fischer, K–1 Teacher
Indianapolis, IN

Sandra Gilbert,
Library Media Specialist
Houston, TX

Angela Leeper,
Educational Consultant
North Carolina Department
of Public Instruction
Raleigh, NC

Pam McDonald, Reading Teacher
Winter Springs, FL

Melinda Murphy,
Library Media Specialist
Houston, TX

Helen Rosenberg, MLS
Chicago, IL

Anna Marie Varakin,
Reading Instructor
Western Maryland College

Some words are shown in bold, **like this.**
You can find them in the picture glossary on page 23.

Contents

Have You Eaten Red Foods? 4

What Are Some Big Red Foods? 6

What Are Some Other Big Red Foods? 8

What Are Some Small Red Foods? 10

What Are Some Other Small Red Foods? . . 12

What Are Some Crunchy Red Foods? 14

What Are Some Soft Red Foods? 16

What Red Foods Can You Drink? 18

Red Fruit Salad Recipe. 20

Quiz. 22

Picture Glossary 23

Note to Parents and Teachers. 24

Answers to Quiz. 24

Index 24

Have You Eaten Red Foods?

Colors are all around you.

You might have eaten some of these colors.

There are red fruits and vegetables.

There are other red foods, too.

What Are Some Big Red Foods?

Some apples are big and red.

The red part of the apple is called the **peel**.

Pomegranates are big and red.

They have a smooth, red skin.

What Are Some Other Big Red Foods?

This **cabbage** is big and red.

It grows above the ground.

This onion is big and red.

The red part grows under
the ground.

What Are Some Small Red Foods?

seeds

Strawberries are small and red.

They have seeds on the outside.

pit

Cherries are small red fruits.

They have seeds inside called **pits.**

What Are Some Other Small Red Foods?

These kidney beans are small and red.

Beans grow on **vines**.

These potatoes are small and red.

They grow under the ground.

What Are Some Crunchy Red Foods?

Some **peppers** are crunchy and red.

Peppers grow on plants.

Radishes are crunchy and red.

They grow under the ground.

What Are Some Soft Red Foods?

Strawberry **jam** is a soft red food.

It is made by cooking strawberries.

Spaghetti sauce is a soft red food.

It is made by cooking tomatoes.

What Red Foods Can You Drink?

Cranberry juice is a red drink.

It is made by pressing juice out of cranberries.

Beet soup is red.

It is made by cooking beets in water.

Red Fruit Salad Recipe

Ask an adult to help you.

First, wash some strawberries, **raspberries,** and cherries.

Cut out the cherry **pits.**

Next, mix everything in a bowl.

Then eat your red fruit salad!

Quiz

Can you name these red foods?

Look for the answers on page 24.

Picture Glossary

beet
page 19

peel
page 6

radish
page 15

cabbage
page 8

pepper
page 14

raspberries
(RAZ-bare-ees)
page 20

cranberries
page 18

pit
pages 11, 20

vine
page 12

jam
page 16

pomegranate
(pom-uh-GRAN-it)
page 7

Note to Parents and Teachers

Reading for information is an important part of a child's literacy development. Learning begins with a question about something. Help children think of themselves as investigators and researchers by encouraging their questions about the world around them. Each chapter in this book begins with a question. Read the question together. Look at the pictures. Talk about what you think the answer might be. Then read the text to find out if your predictions were correct. Think of other questions you could ask about the topic, and discuss where you might find the answers. Assist children in using the picture glossary and the index to practice new vocabulary and research skills.

Index

apples 6
beets 19
cabbage 8
cherries 11, 20
cranberries 18
cranberry juice 18
kidney beans 12
onion 9
peppers 14
pits 11, 20
pomegranates 7
potatoes 13
radishes 15
raspberries 20
spaghetti sauce 17
strawberries 10, 16, 20
strawberry jam 16
vine 12

Answers to quiz on page 22

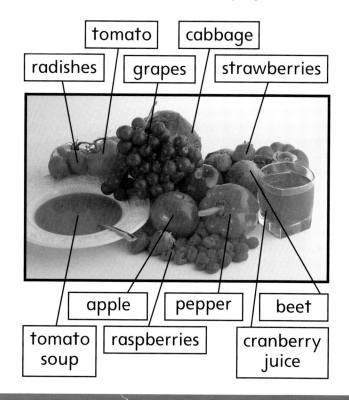

radishes, tomato, grapes, cabbage, strawberries, apple, pepper, beet, tomato soup, raspberries, cranberry juice

24